Life, Liberty, & the Pursuit of Silliness

A Newcomer Comments on Life in Small-Town New England

DOUG BRENDEL
"The Outsidah"

Front cover design: Kristina Brendel
Inspiration: The People of Ipswich, Massachusetts
Back cover photography: Oleg Yarovenko

LIFE, LIBERTY, & THE PURSUIT OF SILLINESS
© 2022 by Doug Brendel
All Rights Reserved

ISBN 978-1-387-90155-5

www.DougBrendel.com
www.NewThing.net

No part of this book may be reproduced or transmitted in any form or by any means, graphic, electronic, or mechanical, including photocopying, recording, taping, or by any information storage retrieval system, without the written permission of the publisher.

Printed in the United States of America

CONTENTS

Silly, isn't it? Yes, mostly

How's your life?

Life isn't just life. There are different types of life. There's public life and private life. Work life and family life. You might be "living the high life"; you might be a low-life. In the old days, people talked about living "the life of Riley." Maybe you live a charmed life, or maybe for you, it's a dog's life.

But of all the lives you could live, there's nothing else quite like small-town life. In fact, if *uniquer* were a word, it would apply to small-town life *in New England*.

Which is where I live. And where I write "The Outsidah," at Outsidah.com. Commentary on life in small-town New England from the standpoint of a newcomer. Which, if you weren't born here, you'll always be.

I didn't start out here. I grew up in the sprawling Chicago area, then spent nearly a quarter-century in the Phoenix megalopolis. So moving to Ipswich, Massachusetts (population 13,000, give or take), some 30 miles up the road from Boston, was like landing on a distant planet. I might have gone into therapy, but instead, I started writing.

Nearly 400 times over the years since then, I've made observations about this phenomenon: *small-town life.*

Yeah, 400 mini-essays, most of which have also appeared as columns in small-town New England newspapers. Sheesh.

I came up in Chicago in the days when great newspapers — the *Tribune*, the *Sun-Times*, the *Daily News* (R.I.P.) — featured famous columnists: Mike Royko, Irv Kupcinet, Siskel & Ebert. People on the train would say, "Did you see what Royko said today?" I wanted to be Royko! I still do. Of course, he wrote 7,500 columns in his lifetime, which puts me some 7,100 behind him. Sure, at the moment, you're still reading, but something tells me you're not going to last another 7,100 rounds of this stuff.

It seemed to me, as a kid, that the columnist life must be glamorous: roaming the territory, observing with brilliant insight, crafting words not only to describe but to inspire. In reality, however, I've mostly been just sitting in my bathrobe in my house and writing whatever comes to mind.

My wife Kristina — who graduated with honors in Literature from the University of Massachusetts, so she should know — observes that my first 400 essays have really been just four essays ceaselessly regurgitated. There's (1) commentary on local traffic, (2) commentary on local weather, (3) commentary local wildlife, and (4) commentary on the byzantine maneuverings of local politics.

I don't prefer to think of "The Outsidah" in such irksome terms. I would say the Outsidah's record is 400 brilliantly variegated essays which have just happened to clump around three utterly captivating themes. With varying results.

For example, in the first 400 outings:

∞ I have interviewed a cigarette-smoking deer, a mosquito on vacation, and a grieving chipmunk widow, and eavesdropped on a squirrel-couple's domestic dispute.

∞ I've insulted the nearby towns of Rowley and Saugus so often, it's become a contest, with prizes, and a parade.

∞ I've been flamed (more than once) for my wisdom about right-of-way on small-town thoroughfares.

∞ I've publicly accused a Town Manager of stealing my garbage can. (Charges were later dropped.)

∞ I've offered major public-service reporting, like my exposé on feral chickens.

And so on. You can sense how I've contributed to the quality of life around here, right?

I've commented on and survived countless nor'easters, potholes, and lawn-watering bans — and weathered multiple local elections and Town Meetings — all, I'm happy to say, without losing more than a couple hundred friends. The Outsidah has had something to say about New Hampshire drivers, cell phones in church, the vending machine at Town Hall, and dog poop.

If you live in a small town, especially in the Northeast ... or if you *previously* lived in a small town ... or if you know anyone in a small town who *loves* it ... or even if they ceaselessly complain about it ... this book may offer valuable insights. Or at least a few moments of painless diversion.

Yes, it's been mostly silliness. There are far more important things in life than whether Topsfield wins the Chowderfest competition. So today, I'm trying to have it both ways: chuckling about life in small-town New England AND doing something meaningful. Here's how:

This book, *Where You From?*, is a selection of — if not the funniest essays, then at least the least lackluster essays, of the first 400. And **all profits from this book go to NewThing.net, a humanitarian charity that my wife and I** lead in the former USSR. See how we're turning this into something meaningful?

NewThing.net provides practical care and support for orphans, abused and abandoned children, children in foster care, the homeless, the disabled, the elderly, hospital patients, and many others in the Republic of Belarus. And because we're all-volunteer on the U.S. side, every penny donated to NewThing.net actually goes into Belarus.

This is deeply rewarding work — and it's *important*. Way more important than this "Outsidah" baloney. Check out NewThing.net. You can even sign up for free photo reports, to visit the former Soviet Union without ever leaving home!

Questions, comments, complaints, hate mail, and/or snarky rejoinders will be happily received; just email Unconventional @DougBrendel.com. Also feel free to send up to 7,100 ideas for new essays.

Doug Brendel
Linebrook Road
Ipswich, Massachusetts

Deer, Me

So I said to the deer, in my backyard, "You okay?"

It was only a courtesy, on my part. She looked entirely okay to me. Like all the other deer who frequent my small-town New England backyard. Well fed. They eat the hostas in my garden. There seem to be enough hostas in my garden to supply the entire local deer population on an annual basis. The hostas keep coming up, the deer keep eating them, and I have yet to find a deer dead of malnutrition in my backyard.

This deer seemed comfortable. Not nervous at all. I think they know by now that I won't take action against them, even though they don't legally have any claim to my property. (At one point I tried to take a doe to court to share a portion of my tax burden, but her clever lawyer used that weepy "Bambi defense," and I didn't have a chance with the jury.)

So I tried to be casual, and friendly, to this deer. She was lounging at my backyard pub table, under my umbrella. Sitting on one of my bar stools, with one of her hooves propped up on the next stool. Her fat, hosta-stuffed belly was protruding unpleasantly. But was I going to comment on this? No. I'm trying to be a good neighbor.

"You okay?" I asked her.

She looked at me with that look. You know, that look that deer give you. I don't mean that "deer in the headlights" look, because this was about 5 p.m. so it wasn't even dark. No. She was giving me that other look. It's the look that deer give you when you encounter them in broad daylight. They sort of lower their eyelids and seem to give you a sneer. They look at you as if to say, "What are *you* doing here? You're a nuisance. Your very presence forces me to put my annoying hair-trigger nervous system on alert. Why don't you just go away?"

You know this look. If you have a teenage daughter, you certainly know this look.

"You okay?" I asked the deer.

She leaned back sullenly on the bar stool, tapping her cigarette into an ashtray on my pub table.

"Don't like that sign," she muttered.

"What sign?" I asked.

She cocked her head toward the street.

"Deer Crossing," she rasped, and took a drag on her Virginia Slim.

I know the sign well. Yellow, diamond-shaped. Silhouette of a deer jumping across the road.

"You have a problem with the sign?" I asked her.

She sighed heavily and took another swig of her Budweiser.

"I don't like where they make us cross," she finally grumbled.

I didn't know what to say.

"Why do you think cars keep hitting deer?" she demanded. "Because they make us cross at the worst possible places." She crushed her butt. "I've lost three cousins on this road alone. Every one of them was crossing legally, right at the sign."

She looked away.

I took a breath. "I think they put the signs up where the deer *want* to cross," I ventured weakly.

The doe snorted. "Sure they do," she grunted. "You think I don't want to cross at the light? But no. Ipswich has me crossing in the kill zone. Thanks." She drained her Bud. "Thanks a lot."

I gulped.

"This town is hell for deer," she murmured.

She swung her leg down and stood up from the chair. "Gotta go," she said, heading toward the road without looking back. "Rush hour. Wish me luck."

Welcome to the Talking House

My house in Arizona was so new, so 90s, so George H.W. Bush, so quiet. All square and fitted and plastic.

My house in Ipswich, Massachusetts, is not George Bush. It's not even Grover Cleveland. It's Adams and Monroe. Half of it was a small barn, built in 1797, the year John Adams became president. The other half is a "Federalist," built in 1817, the year James Madison retired and James Monroe took over. In each half, there's an upstairs and a downstairs, an Upper and a Lower. ("Honey, where are you?" "Upper Monroe!")

An Adams-and-Monroe house is old, sure, but not very old at all by the standards of some people in this town. People who live in 1685 houses on High Street drive past my cobbled-together 1817 house and snort with derision at the white Historical Commission plaque hanging next to my front door. "1817! New construction! Pretender!"

My house is, however, old enough to talk. Literally. You walk through it, and it speaks to you. It creaks or grunts or giggles, depending on the condition of the wood under your feet or the threshold you're crossing. No sneaking around here. And no sleeping in, either: If someone is up and around, you hear them.

There's actually an advantage to this talkative old place: I can save money on utilities, because I don't really need *lights*. Even in the dark, the house tells you, step by step, where you are.

Let's start out back, at the breezeway door. You push, it refuses to open, you put your shoulder into it, it still refuses to open, you bang your shoulder into it, it finally gives way with a *Whump!* You step into the mudroom, and close the door behind you: *Thomp.* You rub your shoulder.

Two steps to the right — the floor says "Tecka, tecka." You pull on the kitchen door, a thin thing salvaged from the 1600s. "Weeep!" it squeaks as you open it. But then, as you close it behind you, it squeaks a different way: "Tew!"

Now you're in the kitchen, Lower Adams. The wide pine floor says *tum tum tum tum.* Turn left, and the floorboards warn you you're heading toward 1817: "Erp! Erp!" In the little walkway where Adams and Monroe meet, the floor says "Ack, ack." You know you're in the Lower Monroe living room when you hear the floor cry out like a movie damsel: "Eek!" If you have a cruel streak, you can actually bounce a little on that first floorboard and torture her: "Eek! Eek! Eek! Eek! Eek!"

Take a diagonal, cross the living room. A big braided rug under foot keeps the floor quiet: "Hm, hm, hm." But when you step off the rug again, the old pine suddenly carps at you: "Kri-ike!"

At the old original 1817 front door, you turn left to go up a talking staircase. Each step greets you:

Ark! Wook! Pook! (Turn.)

Wah! Frack! Gleek! Wipp! Wipperipper! (Loose board, I guess.) *Bick! Kip!* (Turn.)

The last three steps are unenthusiastic: *Kruck. Toop. Bluck.*

Now you're in Upper Monroe. Turn left, and you're in the master bedroom. I can tell where I am because the floorboards mock me: "Ooh! Ook! Yeah! Wow!" Not exactly mood-setting.

Turn away from those sardonic slats, hang a right, and head into the bathroom. Flooring: black-and-white tiles, circa 1985. What's under the tile, I have no idea, but whatever it is, it screeches when you walk on it: *Reechah! Reechick! Cheekick!* Hang a left, you're on a small wooden landing connecting 1817 back to 1797. It sounds like a grandfather: "Groak. Brrp." A couple solid 70s-era steps into Upper Adams — my office, carpeted — and only here does the house go silent. Pull a U-turn and take the stairs down to Lower Adams — these steps say *Scrake, scroik, scrake, scroik* — and you're back in the kitchen.

Simple, huh?

Now let's try it with a blindfold.

Pushing 40

It doesn't take long, after you move to Ipswich, Massachusetts, to understand that this town has a pace all its own.

About 40.

That's 40 miles per hour.

No, it doesn't matter that you're on the 25 mph section of my street, Linebrook Road. People there zip past my house doing ... eh, let me check my radar ... about 40.

It also doesn't matter if you're on a little section of State Route 1 that slices across the western end of town, where the speed limit is 50. You can be in a great big hurry, but you're stuck behind someone going ... oh, I would say ... about 40.

When you move to small-town New England, they sneak in while you're asleep and embed a chip in your brain; the very next morning, you're not capable of driving any other speed. The sign says 25? Aw, maybe 40 will be okay. The sign says 50? They can't be serious. I'm driving 40! Yeah, 40: the sensible speed.

Oh yes, as you're approaching the center of a small New England town, you touch the brake. Why? Because the sign tells you to slow down? No. You touch the brake because an elderly fellow is hobbling across Main Street to the liquor store, and you will send him careening to the pavement if you hit him, and if you hit him, you will have to stop and get out of your car for the whole police report thing, and you will wind up on the police log page of next week's local paper. All of which will really, really undermine your speed advantage. And until now — since you've been driving in small-town New England, after all — you've been doing about 40.

Yes, here in Ipswich, there are places where you don't drive 40 … places

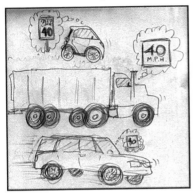

where you drive about 40 the first time, but then you learn not to. The first time you take Washington Street — where the official limit is 30 — you go about 40. You do that once. Then, after your encounter with the potholes, after you get your car out of the shop with your alignment adjusted and your axles welded back into place and your vertebrae re-sequenced, you pick your way along Washington Street like a land mine tester.

But basically, here in Ipswich, we do about 40.

Hello, officer, what seems to be the problem?

Well, do you know how fast you were going?

Yes sir, I was doing about 40.

And do you know what the speed limit is?

Yes sir. I'm an Ipswicher. We go 40.

Oh. Okay, then. Move along.

Crow Tableau

Crows. Are they all over New England? Or just here in Ipswich, Massachusetts? My town is the only one that got the crows?

I lived in Chicago for decades. We didn't have crows in Chicago. We had pigeons. Millions of pigeons. It was pigeon paradise.

In that city's vast public plazas — sprawling rectangles of concrete punctuated by enormous, puzzling sculptures, places where you were supposed to saunter about, or make out on park benches, or eat your sack lunch on a sunny day — pigeons, by their sheer numbers, made all of these options impossible. There was an immense, warbling ash-colored carpet of feathers and beaks and googly eyes, a covering so thick you could hardly walk. If you could get space on a park bench, one look at where you'd be sitting and you didn't feel like eating your lunch — Chicago is one enormous pigeon toilet — and even less like smooching your sweetie. It was pointless to wave the pigeons away: a thousand fat gray birds would erupt, flapping and gurgling and bumping into each other, only to settle back down dopily right in front of you again.

From time to time, the city fathers would proclaim a pigeon purge, but these were generally halfhearted gestures. This was Chicago, after all, which means most of those pigeons were on the rolls as Democrats, and essential on Election Day.

I lived in Phoenix for decades, too. We didn't have crows in Phoenix, either. We had roadrunners — just like the cartoon, except that in real life they're even sillier-looking. Roadrunners are incapable of walking. They can stand still, or they can jet. When they want to go somewhere, they lean forward and explode into a high-speed Groucho walk. But without the cigar. And without the mustache. Or the eyebrows, or the glasses. But other than that, it's just like Groucho.

But when I arrived in Ipswich, I didn't find multitudinous masses of pigeons, or the zigzag vapor trails of roadrunners. I did, however, find crows.

This is no measly blackbird. This is no little birdcage-sized birdie. This is a major animal. I would never want to be guilty of exaggerating, but it looks to me like a crow could easily fly off with your schnauzer. My neighbor Tanya is a black belt, but I've had crows in my backyard that I would never bet against in a round of kickboxing against her.

These are formidable fellows. They strike fear in the heart of the uninitiated. I can be in my backyard, minding my own business, when a sinister shadow falls over the land, a shadow like a 737. Then another, then another. The crows are coming. I shiver. Once they're on the ground, they survey the grounds and begin their caustic commentary. You don't have to speak crow to know what they're saying — in spite of their apparent partial deafness.

"What?" "What kind of place is this?" "What's to eat?" "What?" "I hate it here!" "So do I!" "What?" "What in the world are we wasting our time here for?" "What?" "Look at that moron!" "What?" "With the beard!" "What?" "Let's hate him!" "What?"

They stalk about the yard, glowering at the world with such disapproval, I almost feel obligated to do something different, just to seek their favor.

Maybe somehow arrange a better menu for them? I normally toss out stale Meow Mix the cat refuses to eat; perhaps the crow-gods require better. Premium chipmunk cadaver-snacks? Pâté de fish guts?

To live in small-town New England, one must learn to co-exist with the crows. I am learning. I am a crow-ed student.

Five-Way Stop

They tried to warn me.

When you've lived in Arizona for most of two and a half decades, and you tell a friend that you're moving to Massachusetts, first their face snaps around to see if you're joking, then they frown because the look on your face tells them that you're not joking, and then their mouth opens — a look which I now recognize as cod. ("Close your mouth, Michael," Mary Poppins said; "we are not a codfish.")

And then, after a certain amount of stuttering, your friend typically starts in with the warnings.

They warn you about the Massachusetts weather. The politics. High taxes and liberal churches and — horror of horrors — universal health care.

But most of all, they warn you about the traffic.

They hear "Massachusetts" and they think "Boston." Boston traffic! Shoot me now!

And of course, they're somewhat correct. Boston traffic is, shall we say, intense. I have a very small car, yet somehow, when I drive in Boston, I manage to be in everyone's way. They honk at me, they yell at me. I am a nuisance to them. When they're driving 80 mph in a 35 mph zone, and I'm doing my best to keep up with them, they still hate me. On the other hand, when I'm standing stock-still, or barely inching along in the colossal crush of cars — someone still finds a way to be upset by the lane I've chosen, or insulted by my decision to switch lanes, or disgusted by the fact that I simply exist at all, because apparently I've taken the space that someone worthier could have been occupying.

However, my friends "back west" are wrong to generalize about Massachusetts traffic on the basis of their few rare experiences with Boston traffic. This is not Boston. This is the town of Ipswich. We live by a much different code. We are small. We are human.

So we have decided to overdo it in the opposite direction.

You come to a stop at an intersection in Ipswich, and you look to see if there's anyone you can possibly let go before you. If there's any question whatsoever, you wave to them, to signal them that you would very much like them to go first. If there's a line of cars behind you, it doesn't matter. If you have the right of way, and it's enormously confusing to the person you're signaling to, that doesn't matter either.

At the intersection we call "Five Corners" in Ipswich Center, trying to turn off of Market Street, I have had 20-minute conversations with the drivers on Central, entirely in hand signals. A partial transcript:

(Wave.) "Go ahead."

(Double wave.) "No, please, you go."

(Flitting fingers.) "No, by all means, go ahead."

(Hand swooping.) "You have the right of way."

(Hand swirling.) "Yes, I know, but I'm nice. This is Ipswich. Please go ahead."

(Triple wave.) "Actually, you have more traffic backed up behind you than I have backed up behind me; so please, go ahead and turn."

(Fingers spread, pushing motion.) "No, I can't; I have invested heavily in this conversation, and if I go ahead, it will somehow communicate to the people waiting behind me that I was a fool for entering into this hand-signaling traffic-law-distorting exercise in the first place; please go ahead; I need you to go ahead; my honor is at stake."

At this point, I finally go ahead and pull out. I don't care who has the right-of-way. The law no longer matters. Here in Ipswich, we are human beings. Traffic laws are for primitive places. Like Boston.

You Can't Get There From Here

My brother-in-law visited from Dallas, and boy was he confused.

He was trying to find his way around by taking note of the numbers on houses. He had this idea that somehow the house number relates to the distance you've already driven from the center of town. Ha! Doesn't he know this is small-town New England? You cannot lay down a scientific grid here — 12 houses per block, 8 blocks per mile; forget about it. We're some of the oldest communities in America (after Masconomet's folks, that is), and nobody back then was thinking about master-planning a house-numbering system. They were just trying to coax enough food out of the ground to survive. (Colonial boy: "Please, Mama! No more clams for dinner, or I'm going to sign on with Masconomet!")

You can no more gauge distance in Ipswich, Massachusetts, using house numbers than you can tell what direction you're going by what street you're on. We're a classic almost-four-centuries-old colonial town; our streets are laid out along the precision routes originally established by skittish deer and wandering cows. If you're going SOUTH on NORTH Main Street, you turn LEFT to get onto SOUTH Main Street. That cow had been drinking.

I sympathize with my desperately confused brother-in-law. I grew up on the grid. On the South Side of Chicago, the streets have romantic names like East 59th Street. Then I moved to Phoenix, where they went Chicago one better. Instead of just one-half of the city being numbered, the entire metropolitan area is numbered. I lived at 15261 North 92nd Place. There is also a 92nd Street, a 92nd Avenue, and a 92nd Drive. If you flunked math like I did, you gotta have GPS just to get to the Dairy Queen.

But in those master-planned cities, with their quadrants and their right-angled street corners, you do have a feel for distances. If you're on the 15200 block, you know you're a mile from the 16000 block — 8 blocks to a mile. You're driving along, glancing at house numbers, and your brain goes *click-click-click-click-click*, continuously calculating your position. In New England, we have a somewhat different situation. You don't look at house numbers to calculate distance. You don't calculate distance at all. You calculate time. How far is it? About 20 minutes. Everything in New England is about 20 minutes.

House numbers will do you no good. If my brother-in-law stayed more than a few days, he'd have a stroke. In my neighborhood, for example, 3 Charlotte Road is next door to 3 Randall Road. How could I explain this to my brother-in-law? I had no words. "Just look away," I said. I think he was beginning to twitch.

Linebrook Road, the street I live on, the longest in town, is also the most extreme example of colonial-era house-numbering. The first guy to build a house on Linebrook called it #1. The first guy to build a house on the other side of the road called it #2. It made sense. You build a house, you look at your neighbor's number, you take the next number. Houses on the north side of the street get the odd numbers, houses on the south side get the even numbers. New England rationality! But in the four intervening centuries, more folks built houses on the north side than on the south side. So my house is in the 400s, and my neighbor across the street is stuck back in the 300s.

And my brother-in-law is still craning his neck, squinting at house numbers, trying to get to the airport.

Caution: Paid Pedestrian Crossing

A small town in New England doesn't have a "downtown," like New York City. A small town in New England has a "center." And it's typically a mess.

Take Ipswich, Massachusetts, for example. In Ipswich Center, at what we call "Five Corners," there are so many ways in and out, on foot or by vehicle, I can't even begin to describe the chaos.

If you need to turn left onto Central Street, you're doomed.

Well, maybe not technically "doomed." But you are probably going to sit there for a long, long time. Long enough to ponder complicated questions like "Am I technically 'doomed'?" Or, "What are the mathematical odds of my getting out there onto Central Street without causing an accident?" In fact, you'll have enough time to figure those odds with a pencil and paper. Using long division. Or using an abacus, if you happen to have an abacus in your cup holder.

In any event, you're going to be there awhile.

However, there is hope. You do have allies in this situation. They're called "pedestrians."

People on foot have enormous power in the Commonwealth of Massachusetts. They can stop Mack trucks in their tracks. Since pedestrians have the right of way — and something like super-powered right of way in designated crosswalks — they can stop traffic without a gesture, without a badge, without even a lawyer.

So your most realistic hope for pulling out into the intersection at Five Corners may be a pedestrian who happens be crossing the street. If you're sitting on Market Street hoping against hope to turn left onto Central, your best friend is the woozy housewife stumbling out of the Pub after a few midday beers and crossing South Main. The moment she sets foot on asphalt, traffic moving toward Five Corners from all six possible directions comes to a nervous halt. This is how 18.7% of all drivers in Ipswich get across Five Corners.

Which means, what we need, to alleviate traffic congestion at Five Corners, is street-crossers. (Not street-walkers. Not cross-dressers. Please read carefully.)

Here's how the street-crossers program works.

1. When you subscribe, you get a little transponder to affix to your windshield, just behind your rear-view mirror, next to your EZ-Pass box.

2. As you approach Five Corners, your transponder sends a signal to one of the street-crossers I have hired for your convenience. They'll be stationed at the ten corners we so fondly refer to as Five Corners. Each of them will have a little unit that lights up and vibrates, like the thingy you get from the hostess at a tacky chain restaurant when you have to wait for a table.

3. The moment the street-crosser gets the signal, they'll start crossing the street.

4. Traffic will grind to a halt.

5. You'll be able to ease your vehicle forward, and by the time my street-crosser has street-crossed, you'll be too far out into the intersection to be denied a place in the stream of traffic.

6. Proceed, with snickering.

If the subscription program is successful, we'll add kiosks at certain points leading toward Five Corners, where non-subscribers can get in on the fun. For example, approach from the west and there will be station where you can pull to the curb, pay $5 (cash, please), then immediately proceed to Five Corners. There, a street-crosser will ensure your smooth passage by walking right in front of that Congregationalist SUV trying to sneak across from North Main Street after a chili cook-off at First Church.

As a public service, I intend to hire young people as street-crossers. Young people are the bravest demographic group, and this is, after all, a stepping-out-into-traffic sort of job. After the business is well established — and assuming no young people have been mowed down by inattentive Hummer-drivers, leading to colossal lawsuits and legal fees — we will begin hiring senior citizens. I'm thinking a senior citizen with a particularly problematic hip could be a hero in this scenario. You not only get through Five Corners yourself, but you make all the other cars wait a really, really long time. This could be the basis of a Premium Club membership option.

Please join.

If You Said What I Heard You Say

I hear you.

I don't mean I'm tuned in to you spiritually or anything like that.

I mean I hear you. On the street. Outside my window.

When I moved to small-town New England from modern America, I was not only delighted by the number of old houses in my new hometown, but also shocked by how close they sit to the street.

In the old days, building a house far from the road would have seemed crazy, I guess. If you don't have a Toyota to get you from the house to the street, and you don't have a snowplow service to magically clear a mile of driveway, why wouldn't you simplify your life by plopping your house down right at the edge of the road? Besides, there was no *Colonial Idol* on TV to entertain you, and no sitting in front of ye olde compewter on Ye Olde Facebooke: so you *wanted* to hear the clip-clop of an approaching horse. Visitors! Something new and interesting!

My house, for example, reflects these priorities. There was a small barn,

built about the time George Washington retired, a reasonable distance from the road. But then, about the time James Madison retired, the owner decided to attach a new house to the barn. Hm, where shall we put the new house? Which side of the barn should it go on? By Jove, I've got it! We'll squeeze it in between the barn and the road! So when you step out of the front door, you're in the southbound lane dodging Harleys!

My wife has gently, lovingly suggested that I sometimes exaggerate, so let me assure you, I don't mean to exaggerate about the proximity of our house to our street. Let me simply say that our front yard is the width of a garden hose. You could unspool a roll of Charmin and conceal our front yard completely.

So no wonder I hear you.

On beautiful New England evenings, when the weather is so lovely, I want to open my windows, leave them open overnight. And on beautiful New England mornings, when the sun is up so early, you want to get out, get some exercise. So I don't need to set an alarm for the morning. I have you. Outside my window.

Runners tend to be solo, and all you hear is their feet: *thup thup thup thup thup thup thup thup.* Bicyclists come in pairs, usually men, moving fast — and THEY YELL AT EACH OTHER! So, early in the morning, I hear extremely quick, amazingly loud snippets of stories as the bicyclists zip by:

"...HER, MAN! SHE'S GONNA SHAFT YOU..."

"...GET CAUGHT, BUT HE WAS CRAZED..."

"...DEAL WITH THE PROSTATE THING, SO..."

But best of all are the walkers. They're more often women, and they chatter — they're up at dawn, after all, and full of energy — and they think these historic houses they're walking past are museums; the idea that people actually live here, and might be sleeping at this ungodly hour of the morning, never crosses their mind.

Plus, because they're moving so much more slowly than the bicyclists, they spend significantly more time within earshot — which means I get way, way more information than I want:

"...ridiculous! So something had to give. Finally I just told him, this is not right. If I don't get this baby weaned I'm going to scream! What in the..."

"...don't know if it's love. I like him. He's really nice to me. But I like Paul too. Actually I like Paul better. Or maybe it was the margaritas, I don't know. How..."

Really slow walkers — the ones who aren't serious about exercise — offer the longest monologues:

"...said stop! He wouldn't stop. I grabbed his arm, I said stop it! He was like, what, are you gonna call the cops? I said, give it to me. I had to grab it out of his hand! I said this is not right! This is not the yellow I chose for this room! I actually threw the paintbrush at him. I couldn't believe he was actually..."

Some early morning in the future, groggy and half-awake, I'll hear something really incriminating. Or something really threatening. And I'll have to take action. I'll have to intervene. I'll have to roll out of bed, lean out my window, and sound the alarm:

"Hey! I heard that!"

Banished

That rattling in the ceiling?

That's squirrels, skittering about in the attic of my antique house, living up there without even offering to pay rent or do any of the household chores.

16

I wonder how they got in there, until I notice a gaping hole chewed in one corner of my roof. A ragged aperture, and growing. Where once there was a beautiful angle, the roof pleasingly connecting to the exterior wall in the style of the era — now the point of connection is ragged, an open scab on my beloved 1817 Federal Period house. *Hee hee!* the squirrels seem to snicker. *We've bitten a hole in your history!*

How to fight back? I am helpless. My primary experience with squirrels is *tsk-tsk*ing as I drive by their squashed carcasses on Linebrook Road. ("Too bad," my heathen side mutters. Then my religious side takes over: "Give rest, Lord, to the soul of Your servant [insert squirrel's name here] who has fallen asleep, where there is no pain, sorrow or suffering. In Your goodness and love for all, pardon all the sins he [she] has committed in thought word or deed, for there is no [squirrel] who lives and sins not. Amen.")

In my besieged home, I need help. My squirrel-squatters are eating my

mortgaged wood; they have apparently failed to qualify for food stamps. My domicile is being decimated, nibble by nibble. I need a pest professional. A varmint vanquisher.

The uniformed professional who pulls into my driveway is nonchalant. He shrugs. He has fought this evil before, and prevailed. He is armed not with a gun or a poison, but with a small, squirrel-sized door. He climbs up a very tall ladder and affixes the door over the dreadful defect.

But this is no ordinary door. This door only opens one way: *out*. A squirrel can leave the comfy confines of my attic, but when he tries to return....

"Honey, I'm home!"

(Skittering and scratching sounds from inside.)

"Honey, it's locked!"

(More squirrel sounds.)

"Honey, come on. Open up."

"Harold? Is that you?"

"What do you mean, 'Harold, is that you'? Do you normally have guys coming to visit you when I'm not home?"

"Harold, why are you outside? Come in the house!"

"I'm trying to tell you, woman! I'm locked out!"

"Oh, for Pete's sake. I didn't lock the door."

"Will you please just open it?"

"It opened just fine when you left for work this morning."

"I know that! But it doesn't seem to be working now!"

(Skittering sounds. The door swings open. She steps out.)

"Look. It works perfectly. You are so squirrelly."

"Thanks a lot. I love you too."

(The door slams behind her.)

"Oh, great. Bang on the door. The kids can let us in."

"The kids went to the park."

(They stare at each other for a long moment.)

"This is how it went for Adam and Eve too, isn't it."

"I hate moving."

Going, Going, Not Going

If you are uneasy about reading things related to "going to the bathroom," please, stop reading now. This is about "going to the bathroom."

I don't mean this biologically. I'm not talking about bodily functions. I'm just talking about walking. Starting out at the edge of your bed, which is where you're sitting when you realize you need to go to the bathroom, and then walking, from your bed, to your bathroom.

It should be a simple matter. But this is New England.

New England is the land of blocked-off doorways. In our antique houses, with our nooks and crannies and rooms added on 180 years after the house was built, we wind up with doors where we don't need them. Yet there's a certain Yankee reluctance to spend the time, energy, and money it would take to make it just a plain wall, when there's a chance that in 60 or 70 years, you'll want a doorway there again. So it's not uncommon to see a couch in front of a door, or a chair or a lamp or a table in front of a door – and the owners don't even think of it as a door anymore. It's just a wall that seems to look like a door. Yes, it was a doorway, with people actually walking through it, from James Knox Polk to Millard Fillmore, and again from Grover Cleveland to Warren G. Harding. But the whole rest of the time, basically it's just been a wall.

There's one room in our house where this becomes really serious business. After 200 years of nook-adding and cranny-shifting and space-narrowing and corridor-widening, our house has ended up with one tiny room which has not a single window, but four doors. From this little roomlet, you can get to the guest room, the laundry room, the living room, or a bent little passageway too small to be called a hall. The room is all doors. There is only one precious wall where you can put a piece of furniture without worrying about who will be entering, exiting, bumping, slamming, or otherwise ricocheting through.

What to do with such an odd little place? We are not big TV watchers, so we stuck our TV in here. There's really no other use for this space. Well, this isn't quite true. I have indeed used this odd little room for something else. A single, simple function.

I walk through it on my way to the bathroom.

I abandoned the upstairs bathroom because — I trust it's not too sexist to say — it was overrun by females. As the only guy in the household, I took ownership of the downstairs bathroom. Getting there and back was no problem at all. Until I went out of town for a couple weeks, and my wife decided to rearrange the furniture in the odd little TV room.

So now, instead of slipping downstairs and heading straight to the bathroom, with only one little sidestep along the way — well, that sidestep is now a closed door with a brown couch standing guard in front of it.

Which means, from my bed, I cross the room diagonally, out the bedroom door, hang a right on the landing, down three stairsteps, left, seven more steps, another left, last three stairs, then a right, diagonally across the living room, into the kitchen, wide arc around the table and chairs, into the bent little passageway too small to be called a hall, sharp left, one step into the accursed TV room (making a certain gesture toward the brown couch), hang a left into the laundry room hallway, and a sharp right into the bathroom.

I am planning today to go to the bathroom on Tuesday. Packing a light lunch for the trip.

Ant Can't Rant

Those large black ants? The solitary ones you've seen in your kitchen this spring, marching alone across the counter from the fridge to the sink?

Those are carpenter ants.

Let me assure you, they're not called carpenters because they "measure twice and cut once."

These guys infest anything wooden — say, your 200-year-old house, or your newly installed Home Depot tool shed.

They like to hollow out great cavernous "galleries," and extensive tunnels to get there, in your wooden structure, especially where there's moisture. Like under your window. Or under your deck, your porch, the eaves of your roof. They don't eat the moist, chewy wood, like a termite. They just bite off the wood, tiny-little-ant-sized-mouthful by tiny-little-ant-sized-mouthful, and spit it out, and then do it again. And again. Until one day, your house groans lugubriously and caves in on itself.

What carpenter ants *do* eat is gross: They feed mostly on dead insects. (One favorite snack: sucking the bodily fluids out of a dead bug head.) But they send out scouts to find these tasty morsels, and if the scout's route happens to take him through your kitchen, you may soon have a caravan of carpenters climbing your coffee pot.

"Hold on a minute," I said to one the other day.

"What?" the ant shot back, barely pausing between the knife rack and the Cuisinart. "I'm busy."

"Do you realize this is my house you're in?"

"Eh, I'm just a scout," the ant replied with a sneer. "I'm not stealing your precious Lucky Charms."

"Yeah, but you're casing the joint for your accomplices!"

The ant sat down grumpily on his bulbous posterior metasoma and crossed two of his legs. "Look. It's a job. I bring them the information, and what they do with it is their business. I can't take responsibility for the actions of every ant in the colony. Do you check the politics of your car mechanic?"

He pulled a single strand of tobacco out of his tiny backpack. "Got a light?"

"No smoking. House rule," I muttered. "My wife would kill you."

"Your wife would kill me anyway," the ant sniggered. "Come on, gimme a light. Haven't you ever heard of the 'one last cigarette' tradition?"

I didn't like the way he kept changing the subject.

"You realize what thin ice you're skating on, don't you?" I demanded. "If we see you, we squish you. You're not a very fast species."

"Yeah, I put in for rollerblades, but...." He rolled his eyes. "Budget cuts, ya know."

I snorted. Then I was embarrassed and pulled out a handkerchief and tried to pretend to be blowing my nose.

"Look," the ant continued, "I'm union. I do what I'm told. The contract we negotiated is very fair, in my opinion. I use biochemical pheromones to mark the shortest path from the nest to the food source. Which in your case is from just under the southwest corner of your screen porch — to that bag of tortilla chips you accidentally tore too far down the side."

I choked. Then I was embarrassed and tried to pretend it was a simple cough.

"Once we get the foraging trail established," the ant went on, pausing to yawn a tiny yawn, "my work is done. I move to the next house on my job list."

He pulled out a tiny iPad and perused the screen.

"Chris and Tammy. Three small kids. *Plenty* of food sources."

I summoned my shame and rage in an effort to get back on the offensive.

"But you're not the only one at risk, cutting through my kitchen like this," I growled. "We have another house rule, here at the Brendels': When we kill a carpenter ant, we count. If we get up to seven in a single day, we call the exterminator. Once he comes in, your whole gang goes down."

The ant shrugged four of his shoulders. "You think we don't know all this?" He shook his clypeus with a glare of contempt. "We know your house rule. We can hear, ya know. 'Seven in a day.'" He grunted with derision. "Have you gotten up to seven yet?"

"Well, no."

"Of course not, dummy." He smugly folded his antennae together. "Because we only send out six scouts a day."

I had no retort for this.

So I squished him with my thumb.

"Honey," I called to my wife, "phone the bug guys."

Cover Me

You take the woman you love to the beach. This is half the reason for moving to coastal New England in the first place. (The other half is Town Meetings. Love those things. I think they should be quarterly.)

So you take your woman to the beach. Especially on a cool, cloudy day, when hardly anybody else is there.

But you do not wear shoes. And you certainly do not wear socks with your shoes. No self-respecting beachcomber wears shoes to the beach, let alone shoes and socks.

It's not easy being a nerd.

I grew up in Chicago. You don't go barefoot in Chicago. You have to protect yourself against the jagged shards of a thousand shattered wine bottles and the venomous needle points of a million discarded syringes. At least you did in my neighborhood. Not everywhere, of course. Just on the sidewalks. And on the basketball courts.

I thought my shoes were okay for the beach. I heard someone call them "deck shoes," and the boardwalks (which take you from the parking lot over the protected dunes to the beach) are really just long, skinny decks. The signs actually encourage you to use "footwear" on the boardwalk, because there's a risk of splinters. Footwear! Shoes are footwear! (And don't talk to me about flip-flops. Flip-flops are an abomination. No nagging little stem of rubber is going to ride between my toes, no sir. It's unnatural. It's shoes for me. Shoes all the way.)

But shoes are meant to be worn with socks. Sophisticated people do not wear shoes without socks. I grew up painfully average, longing to be sophisticated; so I never got into the tacky habit of wearing shoes without socks. Accordingly, when I went to the beach with the woman I love, I was, I confess, wearing shoes, and yes, I confess, I was also wearing socks.

Just over the boardwalk, she deposited her sandals near the edge of the dune grass. If she expected me to leave my shoes and socks there, she had another think coming. In Chicago you don't leave your shoes anywhere. You go to a beach on Lake Michigan and leave your shoes, and they're in a pawn shop window by the time you come looking for them.

So there she was, the woman I love, sauntering along the water's edge, in her lovely bare feet, and perhaps glancing from time to time at my shoes, and my socks, and my long pants — oh, wait. Did I mention my long pants? Look, my mother raised me to be careful. You never know when a sudden squall will come up, and you'll wish you had long pants. And a hoodie. It doesn't matter that it's 70 and sunny. Things change fast in coastal New England.

My wife did make me leave my hoodie in the car.

It was a lovely stroll. Of course, she wanted to saunter through the shallows, and I wanted to stay up where the sand was firm, and if you're holding hands, you can't have it both ways. So much for holding hands. Remove my shoes and my socks, and actually *carry* them? The thought never entered my mind.

I would have gotten away with the shoes and socks, I do believe, if it hadn't been for the tide. As the tide goes out, it often forms long rivulets, streams cutting through the sand from the upper beach to the receding bay. These rivulets form pretty quickly, and widen even more quickly, and deepen as they widen. So maybe you've walked a long way along the water's edge in one direction, and then you turn around to head back — and you find that you've got a series of gushing channels to traverse. If you're barefoot, it's not an issue. But you don't want to get your shoes and socks wet, do you?

All the way back, as we came to each gushing tributary, I was reduced to

 hunting for the narrowest place, then leaping from edge to edge, like a terrified cat. It was an untidy business, as I landed each time in soft, sopping wet sand, which caked all over my nice shoes, and sometimes even got on my nice socks.

"You could take off your shoes," she suggested quietly. I was silently horrified. And I knew she would get her come-uppance when we finally got back to the base of the boardwalk. I was quite sure that by now, her sandals had been stolen.

The sun had come out, and the beach was filling up with people. She had trouble finding her sandals, among the dozens of other pairs there.

Are there no criminals in New England? Does no one recognize quality merchandise?

I love it here. But I am still adjusting.

O Death! Where Is Thy Rodent?

I probably should not have attended. Just because you feel badly about the "dear departed" does not necessarily mean it's appropriate for you to show up at the funeral. For example, if you happen to have some measure of responsibility for the dear departed's departure.

Which in this case, I guess I did.

I did not personally assassinate the chipmunk. My cat did the deed. My cat, Hercules Frank Brendel, is a skilled hunter, but a gentle giant: too much of an innocent to kill what he catches. He faithfully patrols our small-town New England house, inside and out, with an unswerving devotion to a single, simple mission: Any uninvited creature must be chased and caught, then dropped, chased and caught again, then dropped again — over and over, until, inevitably, the weary little critter gets away for good.

Herc's sister, Queen Anne, is in charge of insect invaders. She's too classy to swat at anything bigger than a dragonfly. But Hercules is fiercely efficient at scaring off *Mammalia*, *Reptilia*, and those feathered, winged, egg-laying vertebrates. Herc does not murder the mice. He does not slaughter the snakes. He does not finish off the finches. He just pummels them, like a feline Rocky Stallone, until they decide to go somewhere else.

It's a shame, in a way. Herc has the cool of a hit man. He could make it as a killer, if only he had the instincts to take it all the way. (He seems to have a particular contempt for voles — which doesn't bother me, because so do I.) Herc bounds into the meadow behind our house and emerges with a furry, squirming mouthful. He marches to the part of our backyard that he has designated as his own private Roman Coliseum, and he proceeds to play with his prey. I must say, as a city boy, there's something deeply pleasing about knowing that the rodent being smacked like a soccer ball this afternoon won't be crunching the cashews in my kitchen cabinet tonight.

But this week, Hercules made a little error. He was off his game a bit. He momentarily lost his light touch. Perhaps as he prepared to carry his latest victim out of the meadow and into the backyard, he somehow tripped in the tall grass, or stumbled over a stone. Maybe he was a bit hung over, after staying out too late the night before with the cat from across the street, slurping Sam Adams empties tossed out by rude drivers on Randall Road.

Whatever the reason, Hercules did something unfortunate.

He chomped a chipmunk.

Bit a bit too hard. Crunched a crunch too crunchy. Snapped something in that little guy's anatomy that wasn't designed to snap.

So when Hercules dropped it in the backyard, it went *thunk*.

I've been accused of heartlessness when it comes to wildlife, but this was not an easy moment for me. Chipmunks are cute. Everyone agrees that chipmunks are cute. Whoever thought up "Alvin" was brilliant. So when Hercules marched out of the meadow to the Coliseum with a chipmunk in his teeth, I felt a bit of a catch in my throat.

But when I realized the chipmunk had already passed over into that great burrow in the sky ... when I realized that this little guy had stuffed his cheeks with goodies from my garden for the last time ... when I realized that my cat had snuffed out a universally beloved, iconic, cartoonish, delightful symbol of playfulness, cheer, and happy-go-lucky nonchalance...

Well, I had no choice. I had to go to the funeral.

It was a small affair – I mean, the attendees were small. It was a big affair in terms of number of attendees. Clearly the deceased was greatly loved. There in a circle around the grave were his five children from the summer litter; four slightly larger children from the spring litter; ten adult children from last year's litters; nine more from the litters of

the year before last; and of course, one very weary widow. There were lots of little sniffles, and plenty of moist, red-rimmed little eyes, as the little chipmunk clergyman squeaked out some tiny Scriptures.

I stayed well off in the background. I didn't care to be seen at all. Unfortunately, however, just as the service ended – right after the eight little chipmunk pallbearers had lowered the little chipmunk coffin into the ice cream carton-sized hole in the ground – the grieving widow caught a glimpse of me. She never looked away. She turned her steely little eyes on me and marched all the way up to me in her tiny black dress, her tiny black veil quivering with each step of her tiny black Diego di Lucca heels.

"You have some nerve," she rasped.

"I'm sorry," I replied quietly.

"It's too late for apologies," she answered sharply. "You let your cat out. To commit murder."

"I don't think it was technically murder. Murder is intentional. I think this might have only been——" I gulped. "–Chipmunkslaughter."

"Uh huh," she grunted. "Once a cat, always a cat."

She turned and stalked away. For a moment, I didn't move. Then, suddenly, I heard the whirr of sleek feathers cutting through the air. A beautiful blue-gray Cooper's hawk swooped out of nowhere, grasped the chipmunk widow in its talons, and lifted her into the sky without so much as a pause.

The widow shrieked at me as they disappeared together: "I suppose this is your bird, too!"

Antiquated

That creaking you hear? That's Ipswich, Massachusetts. There are more antique houses here than in any other town in the country. In other places, when houses got old, people tore them down and built new ones. Not in Ipswich. I guess tearing something down and replacing it with something else might require a huge Town Meeting debate, and nobody could stand the thought. *Not that! Anything but that! Let's just pound in a few more nails and hold this old place together for another year.*

Of course, to those of us who have come here from newer parts of the country — which, come to think of it, would include just about everywhere — antique houses are a major charm factor. A house with a classic white Ipswich Historical Society plaque on the front is desirable. When I began house-hunting, I couldn't understand why anyone would want something built after Calvin Coolidge — not if you could get a Martin Van Buren! Better yet, in Ipswich you can buy a house that's been lived in since long before anybody had ever even heard of a "president," and the British were still the good guys.

Certainly there are other types of houses here. For example, normal modern houses. These are not for people who cling to the past like I do. These people are normal.

And then there are AINO houses — Antique In Name Only. Houses that still have their original "bones," but you go through the door and *wham!* It's the 21st century. Where the woman of the house once sat softly singing hymns in her lace bonnet and baking bread in a brick fireplace, now there's a PlayStation 5.

But there is another type of Ipswich house. My house. Antique inside and out. Heroically preserved by the previous owner, but still, let's face it: really, really old. Someone took a barn from before George Washington and, just after the War of 1812, added a standard colonial to one end of it. The front of the house leans a bit to the west; the back leans to the east. Or is it the other way around? No two windows hang exactly the same distance from the ceiling. Don't drop anything on the wide pine floors of the kitchen, or whatever you dropped will roll to Rhode Island.

We made the mistake of inviting an antique-house expert to tour the place. In the dirt-floor basement — which could pass for a dungeon in a low-budget movie — he gestured toward the odd assortment of support beams: some wooden, some metal, some actually straight. "This," he announced, "is 200 years of lazy husbands."

But I adore this house. It's not a "First Period," also known as "Colonial" — and it isn't certifiably a "Second Period," or "Georgian" — I guess our house is merely a "Third Period," or "Federal." But this is still better, in my opinion, than, say, a "Fourteenth Period," which is "Ace Hardware." I also prefer it to "Fifteenth Period," also known as "Condo."

I know I'm something of a fanatic. We have retained the squeaking stairs and the jittery banisters and the floorboards that groan when you step on them. We've only updated what we felt we had to — a metal stove in one of the fireplaces, new bricks where old ones were crumbling — but I allowed each revision reluctantly, and I still feel badly about it.

The ghost of the man who built my house came up from the cemetery down the street and visited me one late night not long ago. He floated around awhile, checking out what we'd done to the place.

"This place is creepy," he shuddered.

I Like Bike

Having lived most of my life on concrete sprawls, I never developed a great love of the outdoors. My idea of "roughing it" is stepping down to a *three*-star hotel.

But when we moved to a small town in coastal New England, not so very long ago, it was time to acquire a new lifestyle. The beach! The woods! The greenheads!

So recently, for the first time, my wife and daughter and I tried out a vast, trail-laced state park.

The first trail sign we came across was a heartfelt entreaty, in alarming capital letters:

PEDESTRIANS
PLEASE
15 MPH
SPEED BUMP

I was nonplussed. I have never known a pedestrian to do anything close to 15 mph. I have also never seen a speed bump designed for pedestrians. I could only surmise that this state park has acquired a constituency of really fast walkers. I wasn't worried, however. Since we were on our bicycles, I felt confident that we could run over any pedestrians if necessary, even the 15 mph ones.

We soon decided to leave the paved trails and take on whatever challenge this state park could throw at us. The official contour map suggests that some of these trails are basically level. I can confirm personally that the contour map is a fantasy. This state park's page on Wikipedia is more to be believed. It confirms that "many of the trails over the hills" were constructed "straight up and down slope instead of following the contours." Of course, someone on a horse can take these hills effortlessly, if they don't care about the horse frothing at the mouth. (But watch out for those frothing horses. According to Wikipedia, "The pedestrian is cautioned to be alert for galloping horses and not depend entirely on the alertness of the riders." On the other hand, I was

comforted to see no white crosses situated alongside the trails.)

We soldiered on, and of course, it paid off. We made thrilling discoveries. For example, we found what must be the official Pothole Testing Grounds for the region. This state park has long slopes and wide meadows pocked with rocks and nicks and notches. Descending such an incline on your bike, it's impossible to control your facial muscles. Within seconds, jowls flapping, you're making a kind of *guggity-guggity-guggity* sound. My 12-year-old, with significantly smaller jowls, was more of a *dugga-digga-dugga-digga-dugga-digga*. A fellow passed us coming the opposite way. "Bumpy road, isn't it!" he cried happily. "*Buggada-buggada-buggada!*" My daughter waited till we were a discreet distance past him before turning to me and setting the record straight. "He's wrong," she scoffed. "It's *dugga-digga-dugga-digga-dugga*."

Later, traveling alongside some mushy wetlands, we experienced the joy of encountering actual wildlife.

"Look!" I yelped. "A beaver!"

"Dad, that's a squirrel."

"There! Beaver!"

"Dad, that's a turtle."

"Beaver!"

"Dad, that's a duck's butt."

I found the wildlife to be somewhat deceptive.

Since I had not previously spent a lot of time on bicycles, I realize now, in retrospect, that I probably should have consulted in advance with a bicycling enthusiast. They might have spared me the oddly uncomfortable feeling I had, most of the day, in my lower regions, which I finally realized was the result of my seat being crooked. Not a lot, just 45 degrees or so.

Still, all in all, it was a fine day with the family in the great outdoors, with only the slightest of mishaps.

"Dad! Look! A beaver!

"Dad?

"Mom! Wait up! Dad fell off his bike again."

Raking Lesson

November is somewhat confusing to me. It's not like the Novembers we had when I lived in Scottsdale, Arizona.

First of all, I notice that the trees here in New England have leaves on them. I was not really familiar with leaves in Arizona. Yes, we did have things like trees — spindly, Dr. Seuss-like things sticking up out of the crags, writhing in ultra-slow motion, stretching their thorny fingers toward the brutal sun god, pleading in vain for mercy. These tree-like creatures did not have leaves. They had spines. Spikes. Nasty little pointy things.

But then, as if this were not confusing enough, the leaves here in New England change color. Well, at least, I think they change color. Long-time New Englanders moan interminably at the end of every November: "The leaves hardly changed!" To which I can only reply: Hey, New Englanders, you don't know from "hardly changed." If you want to experience "hardly changed," go to Arizona. Things don't change color in the desert. Unless you count the difference between beige and taupe.

And then — most confusing of all — in New England, the trees begin flinging their leaves to the ground. Where I come from, the spiny prickly pointy things have worked so hard just to grind out an existence, just to draw a few meager droplets of acrid moisture from the sand, there is no way they are going to give anything up. But here in New England, the lindens and honey locusts and pin oaks and sugar maples nod smugly at one another, nonchalantly shrug their branches, and mumble: "Eh, it's November. We don't need these garish old leaves. We'll make fresh green ones — but first, perhaps a winter nap."

End result: a lot of leaves on the ground. By observing my neighbors, I have come to understand that you respond to this situation with something called "raking." I purchased a rake, and I tried this activity. It's quite a bit of work, isn't it! You're actually dragging these increasingly heavy groups of

leaves across the grass, and making piles. Good exercise.

But unnecessary. After a bit of experimenting, I have come to the conclusion that the secret to dealing with fallen leaves is not really raking *per se*. (It's also not about making your teenage son do it. He will be even grumpier than usual.) The secret to dealing with fallen leaves is to wait for a windy day. This being New England, it won't take long. Then you hold the rake with a very light grip, stroke the leaves toward you, lift gently, and sort of flick the rake a bit to release the leaves. If you do it right, your leaves will fly directly into the neighbor's yard. I wish you were here with me right now, so I could show you in person; it would be so much easier than describing it: *Stroke, lift, flick. Stroke, lift, flick.* Get in the proper rhythm, with the wind at 12 mph or more, and you can move an acre of fallen leaves across the street in less than an hour. Two Saturdays ago I inadvertently buried Stella, the neighbors' Jack Russell terrier. I could still hear her yipping, but all you could see was the leaf pile quivering.

I think this might work even better with a leaf blower. Can't wait for next November!

A Three-Hour Tour de Farce

Just sit right back and you'll hear a tale / A tale of a fateful trip / That started from this Ipswich port / Aboard a tiny ship.

My wife and daughter and I decided to rent a canoe and check out the Ipswich River from something other than the road that runs along it at 40 mph.

It's a very simple process: You give a nice-looking fellow your driver's license, and sign your name to a seemingly harmless contract which makes you responsible for nothing more than bringing back the stuff that the nice-looking young man is about to entrust to your care and keeping: one canoe, three life jackets, three square orange floaty seat thingies, and three paddles. Simple enough. You're going to paddle upstream, and then, when you get tired, you turn around and let the current carry you back downstream. When you get back to the rental station, which is situated at the edge of a treacherous waterfall, you simply navigate back to the dock, rather than going over the treacherous waterfall, and you're home free. You get your driver's license back, pay for the time you've spent on the water, go home, and post to Facebook. No problem.

I didn't notice any poster on the wall at the rental station with any information along the lines of "How to Steer a Canoe" or "What to Do If Your Canoe Turns Over." There are some nice brochures available, but they seem to be mostly about how nice Foote Brothers Canoe & Kayak Rental is, and what a lot of interesting things you'll see along the Ipswich River, assuming you stay on or above the surface of it.

I sat in the front, and soon we realized that the person in front is responsible primarily for locomotion. This was okay, because I've been working out with a personal trainer. I figured I would just go into my usual weight-training trance, dreaming of the sound of my own grunting and groaning, and happily pull on those paddles all afternoon.

My wife Kristina sat in the back of the canoe, and soon we realized that she was largely responsible for steering. Also okay. She has been doing this since our wedding day, and thank heaven for it.

Lydia Charlotte, our middle schooler, sat in the middle. It soon became clear that she would be responsible for photographs, and commentary.

Lydia Charlotte wisely brought a waterproof camera. I brought my iPhone. My paranoid wife said I should leave it behind, but if I refused to obey her — because God forbid I should miss a text halfway up the Ipswich River — I should at least seal it in a Zip-Loc bag. Feeling foolish, I put my iPhone in a baggie and sealed it, leaving just a little air in the bag, just in case, har har har, we would later want the baggie to float.

We were doing pretty well until a place where the river narrows and the current picks up and if you're not going straight into the current — let's say you've drifted off to one side or the other, and you're trying to get back out into the middle of the river — well, forget about it.

As we got sideways to the current, the canoe tipped to its left. This was my first indication that the Ipswich River, unlike the high school pool I frequented in Chicago, is unheated.

All three of us were instantly in the water, thrashing around in our life jackets, carried downstream by the current. Kristina, a strong and seasoned swimmer, shouted instructions. For a few panicky moments it was touch-and-go. I labored valiantly to save our daughter's life. I was still laboring valiantly to save our daughter's life as our daughter pulled me from the river.

We were exhausted, sopping wet and goose-bumpy, but glad to be on terra firma. Then, however, the stuff we'd abandoned started appearing from upstream. This, you understand, was stuff that would cost us dearly if we didn't turn it back in to the rental company. So back into the water I went, first to grab the boat, then to grab the paddles, and then to grab the three square orange floaty seat thingies. Oh — and my sunglasses.

When I thought I had finally finished with the rescue operations, so I could begin working on my hypothermia, Lydia Charlotte cried out, pointing frantically toward the water: "Dad!"

My iPhone was floating in a baggie down the Ipswich River.

Back in I went, one more time, dog-paddling like an actual dog, and finally retrieved my precious, fragile connection with civilization. But I quickly discovered that one cannot return to shore with one hand dog-paddling and the other hand holding a baggie up out of the water. I might have held the baggie in my teeth — like a real dog — but I was too proud. And too cold. Also, I was drowning. So by the time I got my iPhone back to the riverbank, the seal had popped, the bag was sopped, and, you might say, the call was dropped. Permanently.

As we trudged back along the path through the trees, sodden and shivering, I was stricken by the realization that I had endangered my young daughter's life. I knew she had been traumatized by the ordeal, emotionally damaged, perhaps forever.  Soon, I was confronted by the truth. She turned to us with one eyebrow arched, a kind of crazy gleam in her eye.

"That was awesome!" she squealed — and went skipping down the path ahead of us.

Apples to Apples, Dust to Dust

There are four apple trees at the back of our property, lined up like dutiful soldiers. Sometimes I refer to them as John, Paul, George, and Ringo. Other times I call them Groucho, Harpo, Chico, and Zeppo. Depending on the season, they can also be the Four Horsemen of the Applocalypse.

When we bought our house in small-town New England, not so very long ago, I would not have known that these four trees were apple trees, because we had no such thing as apple trees in the desert, where I spent the previous two decades. (We had mesquite trees, which are judged not by the quality of their fruit, of which there is none, but by the sharpness of their barbs, which can cut you to the bone while you're attempting to scoot under them to adjust your pool sprinkler.)

But during our New England house-hunting expedition, the selling agent pointed out the four apple trees. They were planted in a prim and perfect row, almost certainly the result of a 1958 middle school science project.

Since the day we bought the house, I have learned that apple trees do not just give you apples, year after year, like mindless droids. Apple trees wax and wane. They give and they withhold. They are operating under some higher authority: maybe God, or the local Zoning Board of Appeals.

So three summers ago, our apple trees decided to go artsy. They sprouted blossoms. Wonderful! Beautiful! They were the Vincent Van Goghs of the tree world. Not a single apple, but plenty of lovely little flowers.

Summer before last, having rested up, our trees exploded with big, beautiful, juicy apples. Thousands of fabulous apples. The ground was like cobblestone, covered with fallen apples. Visiting deer made themselves sick gorging on apples — I saw a doleful doe holding a cool washcloth to the forehead of her puking fawn — and still there were apples. My daughter the apple-lover ate apples around the clock. We had apple pies, apple bread, apple cobbler. We used apples to make cake, chutney, fritters, turnovers. Apple crisp, applesauce, apple butter. Juice, cider. Candy apples. Apple-stuffed everything. I believe at one point we had creamy baked savory-sesame-bacon-onion-cheddar-caramel-mustard-chicken-apple-ginger-fennel-horseradish-slaw-sausage-crepe-sauerkraut fondue. We bought a fruit-drying contraption and learned to make apple chips. We had apple in our oatmeal. In our salads. In our meatloaf. We used apples for decorations. If we could have somehow turned them into fuel, we would have been set for the winter.

In desperation, we put out an all-call to our friends, pleading with them to come pick apples. We left a basket, a long-handled apple-picking tool, and a ladder propped outside our house, so any random stranger could come collect apples without an appointment any time of the day or night. I considered putting up a big sign out on the road: "Maybe you can't pick your neighbors, but you CAN pick your neighbors' apples. *PLEASE*." Only one faithful friend, a rather short woman who lives in the center of town, came to our aid. She took away a mountain of apples taller than herself. And still we were drowning in apples.

Finally, this summer, our temperamental trees for some reason decided to go Goth. All four of them produced the creepiest crop of apples in New England history: black-splotched, misshapen little reddish blobs, their skins hideously cracked to reveal the soft, fleshy domicile of a legion of worms. *Appallus domestica*. Even the deer snorted and turned away.

This year, however, we have no apple problem. Our frightful fruits are being carted off, and it isn't costing us a penny. We learned last week that our next-door neighbor's two children, a kindergartener and his even-younger accomplice of a sister, have been slipping into our yard, snagging apples by the bagful, and proudly delivering these grotesque offerings — as their own family's personal gifts — to all the homes on the street.

These children have come up with a beautifully perfect crime. They sneak, they steal, they lie — and ruin their parents' reputation for classy gift-giving. But at the same time, our meadow is blissfully clear of apples. I love these kids. I hope next year to save the town's $50 curbside fee by getting them to handle my compost.

Shuck the Oysters

If you grew up in the middle of the country, like I did — far from the ocean — there are certain activities in which you should never attempt to engage. They are beyond you. Operating a sailboat, for example. I have never done this. It would be crazy. Practically suicidal. Deep-sea diving. Deep-sea fishing. Deep-sea anything. No way. These are functions intrinsically restricted to natives of the coast. Landlubbers cannot acquire these skills. You can try to learn, but you will fail. In the process, you may endanger yourself and others. I know whereof I speak. Recently, I was foolish enough to engage in one of the actions well known to be off-limits to inlanders. It was my mistake. No Chicagoan should ever try what I tried.

"Shuck some oysters," my wife said.

No problem, I thought. We live in New England now. We can buy oysters, still in their shells, at the local grocery store. If we wish for a dish delish and oysterish, we don't need to pry these delightful delicacies out of a can, or unscrew the lid off a common jar, or beg a friend for help, and slide them all gooey and gray out of a Ziploc bag. We can go straight to nature. We can take the animals live, bring them home — while they still think they're invincible — then slaughter them ourselves, personally, one on one.

Not that I had ever done this myself, you understand.

But it was about time, I figured — in fact, the universe had just given me a sign that I was destined to enter the oyster-shucking season of my life. A couple days earlier, a house guest presented me with a lovely gift: an oyster knife, hand-crafted by her late father. When the oyster-shucker is ready, the oyster knife appears.

Shucking cannot be very hard, I said to myself. For starters, it has a silly-sounding name. *Shucking*, indeed. We don't use a romantic Frenchified term like *écailler* or a euphemism like *releasing*. This is not "deliverance." We don't call it "emancipation." It's shucking. Plain and simple.

My wife made every attempt to advise me. Her own personal history, however, is as shucking-challenged as mine, so I felt no real compulsion to heed her counsel. She was suggesting babyish things like holding the oyster in a dishtowel to protect my hand, and placing the point of the knife in the hinge of the oyster the way beginners do, and twisting the knife a bit to gain leverage rather than applying intense pressure to force my way in. All nonsense, of course.

I stood over my kitchen sink, my face reddening, my hands grappling with that first oyster of the dozen, smoke spurting from my ears. Suddenly the keepsake oyster knife lost its tentative foothold on the creature's crusty lip under the insistent pressure of my clumsy fist. The shell splintered open, and one enormous shard came slashing through my thumb.

Let the record show, it was the shell, not the knife — it was the shuckee, not the instrument of shuckification — that severed so much of my epidermis from my musculature.

And let the record show that my adult son, who happened to be standing nearby, saved my life by running for Band-aids.

It was also my son who wisely went to his iPhone and asked, "How do you shuck an oyster?" Within seconds, Legal Seafood's head chef was offering up a YouTube video on the subject. I must report, sadly, that *le chef* was demonstrating every detail of my wife's previously ignored advice.

So today, I am older, and wiser, and bandaged.

The oysters were scrumptious.

I offer the following as a gift to future generations:

THE OUTSIDAH'S LANDLUBBER OYSTER-SHUCKING GUIDE

PREPARATION: Wear gloves.
EQUIPMENT: Oyster knife. Bandages. Tourniquet.
Oxygen optional.
BONUS NOTE: Watch the YouTube video first.

At First, It Was Only a Couple of Sunflower Seeds

Ever since a horrific coyote assault last year, we keep our surviving cats indoors. As a side-effect, the animal kingdom has expanded its territory. The mice, the voles, the chipmunks, the squirrels, the bunnies, the birdies, and the snakes — all the species once fiercely targeted by our felines — have returned to the premises. They now hop, skitter, twitter, frolic, and slither about the property. They peck, graze, scrounge, and otherwise feed off the land as if God intended it this way. Which I guess he did, at least until he created cats.

We have a fine-looking bird feeder in the backyard, a tiny shingle-roofed cottage with see-through walls, hanging from a shepherd's-crook pole. Back in the days when we still had a backyard Cat Patrol, I felt a little guilty about putting birdseed in the little house. It was like luring our innocent, fine-feathered friends into the Carnival of Death: "Step right up, take your chance, peck the sunflower seed and win a prize!"

Now, however, we can fill the feeder guiltlessly. Our backyard is idyllic, a safe haven for rodents, reptiles, robin red-breasts and their ilk. Our cats sit trapped on the screen porch restlessly observing the wildlife. It's Torture TV.

They meow and lick their lips, tails twitching with primal longing, till they eventually trudge inside the house, throwing me a spiteful glance on the way to their food bowl, where they crabbily crunch their dry, brown Meow Mix.

I felt good about the full feeder until it became a major budget item. I was soon spending more money on birdseed than gasoline. We could fill the little house to the brim on Monday, and by Tuesday it was empty. This didn't seem possible. There aren't enough birds in our backyard to eat that much seed in a week. If the birds were actually consuming that much birdseed, they would be too fat to fly. We should see a literal "round robin" waddling across the grass. We should have house wrens the size of actual houses. But no. All the birds seemed normal-sized.

Squirrels, maybe? Squirrels love birdseed. But we have a big metal cuff, shaped like an upside-down funnel, underneath the bird feeder, designed to deter squirrels; and as far as I can tell, it works. We have plenty of squirrels, but they have no engineering sense. None seem to have figured out how to prop up a ladder, or shoot a guywire from the nearby maple tree, or stack pairs of fallen branches in a criss-cross pattern, or otherwise employ the laws of physics to get to the coveted delicacies.

So where was all the darn birdseed going?

Yesterday I was sitting on my screen porch, tapping my laptop keys, when the mystery was solved. I looked up to see a doe standing at the bird feeder with her tongue sticking out. Not at me — it was extended into the bird feeder's little bird-sized door. Her head was cocked awkwardly to one side in order to get absolutely as much of her tongue as possible into the little house. She was slurping birdseed into her mouth as fast as she could.

I slapped my laptop shut, set it aside, and stood up, knowing that the sudden activity would send the startled animal scampering away. I was wrong. The doe stopped slurping for a moment, eyeing me wearily, then went back to her task.

"Hey! Cut it out!" I barked at her.

She kept an eye on me, but didn't break stride — er, uh, slurp.

I advanced toward the porch door, attempting to appear menacing. Appearing menacing is apparently not my forté. The deer kept at it.

"What the heck!" I exclaimed, stepping outside. I knew she'd run now. I walked up to her. She only slurped faster.

"Get away from my bird feeder!" I yelled, waving my arms.

Finally she pulled her tongue back into her head and straightened up.

"I can quit whenever I want," she said evenly. Then she stuck her tongue back out and started in again.

I burned with shame. I never realized that birdseed is a deer opioid. I was providing the drug — pound after pound of it, day after day — to the addict.

"You have to stop," I said.

"I'm not hurting anyone," she replied between gulps.

"I can't afford it," I answered.

"I knew you'd turn on me," she sneered. "You did this to me. Now you loathe me."

"It was an accident! I didn't know!"

"Is that my problem?" she shrieked.

"You don't need more birdseed!" I cried. "You need help!"

The doe took another slurp. "I'll get help later. Just not right now."

I placed a hand gently on her shoulder. "Listen to yourself," I pleaded.

The doe paused. She backed her nose away from the birdfeeder and peered inside, frowning. It was empty.

She swung her face toward me, and blinked her enormous eyes.

"Got any more?" she asked.

If You Can Hear Me, Tap Three Times

Please help me. Come rescue me. I'm in here, I promise. Somewhere beyond the mudroom. If this message reaches you, please, I beg you, come to my house, find some way, I have no idea how, to get through the mudroom, and haul me out.

I have no idea how this happened, getting barricaded in my own house, by my own stuff. Where I come from, we didn't have mudrooms. In the Arizona desert, we didn't have mud. Mud, as I understand it, is a concoction of dirt and water. Dirt, I get. Over the course of my desert years, I became familiar with a whole range of dirt types. We had sand, grit, gravel, dust. In the urban areas, we had grime, filth, soot, even grunge. Plenty of what you'd call dirt. But hardly ever did we come across dirt combined with water. Because for the most part, the only water we ever saw in Scottsdale, Arizona, was piped in from the often-dry Salt River and carefully restricted to exquisitely profligate fountains out in front of insanely lavish resorts.

Hence, no mud. Hence, no mudrooms.

But moving to New England and shopping for an antique house, I quickly discovered the alternate reality, the fifth-dimensional space, known as the mudroom. It is the humblest of chambers, bearing the humblest of names. The mudroom is never called the "entryway," even though it is a way of entering. God forbid a New Englander should ever call it the "foyer" — that would be way too fancy. Likewise for "reception area." And "vestibule" would be too churchy. No, this is the "mudroom." It's a wretched little cube, tacked on to an otherwise pleasant house, and named for a mixture of water and dirt.

It's also, apparently, magnetic. In my very limited experience living in New England, I find that mudrooms attract junk. Not just metal junk, like a normal magnet. No, mudroom magnetism is eclectic. In the mudrooms of New England, you're liable to find hats and coats and scarves and boots, and whatever tools don't quite fit the current season, and the carrier you take your pet to the vet in. A few valiant folks are diligent enough to keep their mudrooms from accumulating clutter, but they mostly fall into one of two unfortunate categories: they're either haggard from the continuous effort, or totally wired on caffeine, if not something stronger. And if you have school-age children — even just one of them — there is absolutely no hope for your mudroom. You're going to find yourself clambering over an ever-morphing mountain of rubber boots, forgotten schoolbooks, splintered skateboards, and the part of the sandwich they put down to get their mittens on.

I guess it's clear now that I simply couldn't keep up. Or maybe "couldn't" is the wrong word. Maybe I just made bad life choices. Maybe if I had assiduously attended to my mudroom, perhaps just removing a small percentage of the debris each day, say 50 or 60 items, I could have stayed ahead of the buildup. Maybe my priorities were misplaced. If I had spent less time making a living, if I hadn't wasted all those hours caring for my children, or eating right and getting plenty of exercise, I wouldn't find myself in the predicament I'm in today: trapped in my house behind a mass

of assorted objects so intensely packed and intricately interlocked that I can hardly even get a cell signal in here anymore.

It's not as if I could simply advertise a garage sale and hope for neighbors to take this stuff away, item by item, for a dollar apiece. This is not stuff anybody else would want, under any imaginable circumstances. There's rusty barbecue equipment, and the grimy fishing hat that I always used to wear while barbecuing, before I couldn't find the barbecue equipment anymore. There's a Frisbee so warped it won't Fris anymore. There's a square of cardboard with FREE scrawled on it in huge letters, which last year advertised our bumper crop of apples on a table out by the street until someone took all the apples and the table the sign was taped to. There's a hat somebody gave to my wife which she would never wear in a million years. A random light fixture. A spool of kite string knotted beyond redemption. A haggard sweatshirt celebrating the Chicago Bears' 1986 Super Bowl victory. Mounds of various colors and textures of fabric probably constituting clothing from my daughter's fifth-, sixth-, seventh-, and early eighth-grade eras. And innumerable as-yet-unreturned empty milk bottles from a local farmstand. If the price of milk goes up out there, it will be because we have $62,418 worth of their bottle inventory in our mudroom.

So I implore you, if you're reading this, take pity on a poor fool. Bring a Bobcat. Bring a blowtorch. Possibly bring a priest. Whatever you think might help. Get me out of here. I know it won't be easy. But I'm pleading with you on humanitarian grounds. My daughter will graduate in four years, and I want to be there.

Credit Due

Thanks to **Dan MacAlpine** (lovingly depicted at right), longtime editor of the *Ipswich Chronicle* (now the online-only *Chronicle & Transcript*), who got me

started writing these essays, and then couldn't get rid of me.

Thanks to my wife **Kristina Brendel** (badly depicted at left), who serves as "first reader" for every column I produce. She is truly insightful and wise, and her feedback hardly ever makes me cry.

And thanks to my ever-faithful, ever-excellent, ever-patient proofreader, **Sarah Christine Jones** (not depicted here, as a kindness), of Wadsworth, Ohio. She graciously reviewed the original essays. (Please don't hold her responsible for the content.)

Let Us Connect

- Doug's contact info is at **DougBrendel.com**.
- His New England humor blog is **Outsidah.com**.
- His most important stuff is at **NewThing.net**.
- Look for Doug on Facebook (New Thing, Inc.), Instagram (DougBrendelIpswich), Twitter (DougBrendel), and everywhere fine writers are sold.

NEW THING

A Response of the Heart for Belarus

This book was conceived to benefit **New Thing**, the humanitarian-aid charity based in Belarus, in the former USSR, founded and led by Doug and Kristina Brendel.

A team of Belarusian workers devote themselves to bringing hundreds of tons — millions of dollars' worth — of donated food and goods into Belarus each year, sharing this aid face-to-face with people in need from all walks of life, and the workers who give their lives to serving them:

✓ Orphans and foster families
✓ Abused and abandoned children
✓ Children and adults with disabilities
✓ The homeless and poor
✓ Hospital patients, sick kids in other institutions
   And the list goes on.

This work of compassion is **all-volunteer** in the U.S., so every penny you donate goes into Belarus. Any donation to New Thing is eligible for U.S. income-tax deduction to the full extent of the law.

You can visit the former USSR without ever leaving home!

To receive photo reports and updates on New Thing's work in Belarus, simply visit **NewThing.net** and fill out the secure online form.

We'll be happy to hear from you!

Thank you!

And we'd be grateful to have your help. To donate, visit our donation page at **NewThing.net**.

Thanks again!

Please visit us, follow us, like us!
Web: **NewThing.net**
Facebook: **New Thing, Inc.**
Instagram: **NewThingNet**
Twitter: **DougBrendel**
Thank you!

The Plural of *Proviso*, Whatever It Is

1. The material in this book is just Doug Brendel's. He wrote it all as a volunteer, so anything in this book that also appeared elsewhere is Doug's responsibility. Don't blame a newspaper, a website, an app site, or that gossip in the Shaving Needs aisle at the grocery store who insists on telling you all about the Outsidah's most recent outrage.

2. The legendary John Updike (above) might not actually sit in a cloud in heaven and inspire the Outsidah. But just try to prove he doesn't.

3. Ipswich, Massachusetts, inspired the essays in this book, and Ipswich is world-famous for its fried clams, but have no fear, no clams were fried in the printing of this book.

www.DougBrendel.com